D1824074

Greater Than a Tourist – Hamburg

Germany

50 Travel Tips from a Local

> TOURIST

Nicola Coutinho

Lock Haven, PA

ISBN: 9781521725368

>TOURIST

50 TRAVEL TIPS FROM A LOCAL

DEDICATION

This book is dedicated to Kay, my Hamburger for life.

BOOK DESCRIPTION

Are you excited about planning your next trip?

Do you want to try something new while traveling?

Would you like some guidance from a local?

If you answered yes to any of these questions, then this book is just for you.

Greater Than a Tourist- Hamburg, Germany by Nicola Coutinho offers the inside scope on Hamburg. Most travel books tell you how to travel like a tourist. Although there's nothing wrong with that, as a part of the Greater than a Tourist series, this book will give you travel tips from someone who lives at your next travel destination.

In these pages you'll discover local advice that will help you throughout your stay. This book will not tell you exact addresses or store hours but instead will give you an excitement and knowledge from a local that you may not find in other smaller print travel books.   Travel like a local. Slow down, stay in one place, and get to know the people and the culture of a place.

CONTENTS

Author Bio

Nicola Coutinho is a Homoeopathic Consultant from Goa, India. She moved to Hamburg two years ago with the love of her life, whom she met while on a midnight train seven years ago. The city and spirit of Hamburg made her fall in love all over again. When she isn't practicing, or travelling, she devours a book, the dance floor or the basketball court with equal fervor. Yoga, creative writing and West Coast Swing are among her top favorites.

She enjoys backpacking through countries and believes in having more than just a touristy experience. The secret, she says, lies in doing it like a local!

WELCOME TO > TOURIST

WHY AM I A LOCAL?

I wasn't born or raised here. I chose Hamburg. To me, moving here was like being born again. The liveliness, the diversity and the energy of this port city has captured my heart. Living up to its name, "Door to the World," Hamburg flung open the doors to a million possibilities for me.

 The fresh sea-scented air, mix of old and new world architecture and the constant buzzing activity all around is magical. Multi-nationality is one of Hamburg's fortes and there is never a dull moment should you decide to take a walk down to the center or the harbour.

Most importantly, Hamburg opens its arms to you irrespective of whether you are Chinese, African, gay, straight, young, old, Muslim, Christian or any of the many shades of 'different' you can name. I have spent countless hours exploring its nooks and crannies and swear I can help you find the best things to see, do and eat in town.

Herzlich Willkommen!

1. Come Well Prepared

Hamburg has a million things to see, taste, do and experience. It's a good plan to acquaint yourself in advance with tiny tips and tricks so you can make the most of your time here.

Know your route: pick up maps and guide books, mostly free, at tourist centers located at train stations and the airport.

Check the weather forecast: we have rather unpredictable weather so it's good to be prepared with an umbrella or jacket against rain and wind.

Download the official transport App called HVV: it's tremendously helpful to figure out your way around local transport.

2. Start Your Sunday At The Fish Market

The Hamburg Harbour has the perfect place for your Saturday night fever to continue. The Fish market begins as early as 5am (summer) or 6am (winter) on Sunday morning. Bursting with live music, food and drink it's just what you need to keep the party going. A stop at the Reggae Barista cart is a must. Jessy Greaves will have you grooving to the tunes of his aromatic coffees and Rasta beats! Although it's very early, do try a fish bread (check tip 4 for more).

Not the partying kind? Enjoy an exquisite sunrise at the harbour or shop at the little stalls. It's good to know that as the clock inches towards 9:30am, prices drop and offers get more generous.

3. Allow The Water To Inspire You

Hamburg shares an intimate relationship with water and you will immediately see why. Take a stroll down the river Elbe, marvel at the Innenalster- the small inner lake and the far larger Aussenalster- the outer lake. These water bodies are always brimming with action. The city is intersected at every other lane by little canals, which back in the day, were used by sea traders to bring in their wares to the city center.

Along the lakes you often find hungry ducks, sea birds and swans who will readily eat out of your hand. Be careful though, they can be a noisy, rowdy bunch!

4. Do It Like A Fischkopf

People from Hamburg are often called Fischkopf or Fish Head. Want to sound like a local? Learn to use the greeting: Moin, moin! We say this to each other at any time of the day or night. Using it will definitely gain you some points with the locals.

Order a Fischbroetchen or Fish bread- something every true Hamburger relishes.

Good phrases to have in your German kit are: Bitte- please and welcome, Danke schoen- thank you and Ich moechte ein Bier- I would like to have a Bier!

5. Be-er Local

You would do Hamburg a great wrong if you don't taste its local brew-Astra. Sip it at the lake, on the streets or at a Biergarten- a Garden dedicated to drinking Beer- yes we actually have those! The Sternschanze and Altona areas have a few breweries you can visit and make your own beer at.

If you prefer having a shandy, ask for Alsterwasser. Perhaps alcohol is not your thing, try the much-loved Fritz Cola which comes in several different flavours.

6. Bring Your Dancing Shoes

Hamburg has a large scene of dance enthusiasts. Salsa and west coast swing parties happen almost every weekend.

Often in summer, you'll see a live band playing in a park to a wild hip-swinging, foot-tapping crowd.

For those bent towards electro and techno parties, check the scene at Schanze and the Reeperbahn.

7. Walk The Talk

Sign up for a walking tour through Hamburg. There are even free tours that start everyday outside the town hall or Rathaus at 11am and 2pm.

Alternatively try a Bus tour on a hop-on hop-off service which begins at the main train station or Hauptbahnhof. There are still more tour options- cycles, mini cars, electro rollers and of course- just you and your map. I often find getting lost and discovering a new city by yourself has a certain charm to it.

8. Explore The Heart Of The City

The most central part of Hamburg is its majestic town hall or Rathaus and the little streets connecting it to the inner Alster.

Avail of a tour through the inside of the town hall and find out how the symbol of the city evolved over several fires and destructive events, right from the time of the Vikings!

9. Re-Trace The Great Fire Of Hamburg

Find your way to the tiny ally in Deichstrasse where it all began, until its merciful end at a street called Brandsende (fire's end) near the main station. Learn of the many rumors surrounding the fire of 1842 and how it destroyed a third of the city.

What fascinates me is how several buildings, including the Rathaus were blown up in an attempt to contain the fire! I'll let you find out for yourself how that went.

10. Find A Place To Crash

Your options are many and varied. My only request is book in advance or you could be disappointed. Swing by fancy places like the Empire Riverside Hotel or the Four Seasons; book a budget place like Generator Hostels or Backpacker St. Pauli. Alternatively stay at a local's house using Couchsurfing or Airbnb.

"Twenty years from now you will be more disappointed by the things you didn't do than by the ones you did do." – Mark Twain

11. Take Home A Piece Of Hamburg

Souvenir shops offer a variety of options to choose from. For those looking at something off the usual path- pick up an Anchor- a symbol many Hamburgers identify with, a sample of soil from the river banks, a local food or drink so your memories may be re-lived or St. Pauli knick-knacks. Shopping at a local shop or market is often more reasonable than doing so at a tourist location.

12. Dig Into A Plate Of Labskaus

This interesting mixture of foods while not so pleasing to the eye is considered a staple food of seamen. The origins date back to poor sailors lumping whatever food was available to them into a tasty dish. The result- mashed salty beef, onions, potatoes, red beets; topped with fried eggs and pickles and garnished with Herring. Go on, give it a taste!

13. See The Elphi

The Elbphilharmonie, is a dazzling concert hall located in Hafen City on the river Elbe. It is said to be an acoustic wonder and one of the best of its kind world over. The Elphi is a must when you are in Hamburg. Attend a fancy concert, take a guided tour or simply avail of the free entry to the plaza and enjoy a fantastic view of the city from your high post.

14. Go Church Hopping

Churches that survived the fire and World Wars speak of a past that had hard times, harder workers and a big talent. St. Peter's Church or Petri Kirche has a remarkable history starting at its very doorstep. There are often free concerts one can attend in the evenings.

St. Nikolaikirche or St. Nicholas' Church is now almost in ruins but has a beautiful memorial attached. Every hour, the bells chime melodiously and seem to transport you to a long forgotten world.

St. Michael's Church, Hauptkirche Sankt Michaelis, colloquially called Michel is a prominent feature of Hamburg's skyline. The 132-meter-high spire is a landmark for ships sailing up the Elbe. Soak up history and relish an unrestricted view of the city from the very top!

15. Stroll Along Landungsbruecken

Get to this harbour side street by the U 3 tube and drink in port atmosphere. You have a beautiful view to enjoy and a whole stretch to walk along. You will pass a popular beach area called Strand Pauli, lots of kiosks and the Portuguese quarter where you may relish authentic Portuguese food.

As a plus point, Hafen City is a hop skip and jump from where you are.

16. Visit A UNESCO Heritage Site

Speicherstadt or City of Warehouses, located in Hafen City is the largest of its kind in the world. The buildings rest on a base of wood, mostly oak. This area was originally built as a custom free zone for transport of goods. Since 2015, Speicherstadt has been awarded UNESCO Heritage site status. It is also home to several visit-worthy museums such as the Zoll (tax) Museum and Hamburg Dungeon (an interactive tour through the dark past).

17. Set Aside Time For Museums

You're in the right place! With over 70 fabulous museums and galleries,  here are two which you may not find in a usual tourist book.

Deutsches Zusatzstoff Museum/German Additives Museum- a terrifying display of added ingredients in our food which don't belong in our bodies.

One Zero More- an alternative art gallery that you have to work hard to find in the tiny allies of Altona.

Besides these, you may want to check out the Maritime Museum, Miniatur Wunderland, Chocoversum and the Coffee Museum.

18. Explore The Rote Flora

The one graffiti covered, run down building in Hamburg that has resisted the tests of fire, violence, police and governance. The Rote Flora has been occupied by punks, squatters, leftists and the homeless since 1989. All attempts at re-taking the place have failed through sheer rebellion. It is a symbol of the radical Left in Germany. Today there are art shows and concerts hosted at the portals of this defiant structure.

19. Discover A Magical Musical

People from all over Germany come to Hamburg to watch Musicals. Find out which one is on while you are here and have the time of your life! Although they are in German, it's definitely worth a visit. Music and dance transcend language barriers and let magic come alive.

Some of the musicals we've had so far are The Lion King, Aladdin and the Magic Lamp and Billy Elliot.

20. Treat Yourself To Street Food

Sink your senses into a Bratwurst: fried sausage in bread, a Currywurst: sausage peppered with spiced powder and tomato sauce, a Doener- a Turkish delight of meat, salad and bread or simply some Pommes- Fries. Give two more a shot: Kumpir- baked, stuffed potato and Croques-a French sandwich with a Hamburg touch. Additionally, Hamburg offers you cuisines from around the world, so foodies; you're in for the time of your life!!

"Once the Travel bug bites, there is no known antidote, and I know that I shall be happily infected until the end of my life!" -Michael Plain

21. Beach Out At Blankanese

Known as one of Europe's most affluent areas, Blankanese has a charm of its own. Walk along its sandy shores, sip on a warm drink while a ship thunders by and soak in a magical sunset if the weather gods are kind to you.

If you walk 300 meters or so down the beach and past the lighthouse, you will find shipwrecks. The remnants of submarines and a destroyed schooner now form a breakwater.

22. Get Star Struck

Hamburg's Planetarium is unique in that it is situated in an old water tower and is one of the oldest in the world.

Recently renovated, it boasts of state of the art technology. Rest assured that a show here will give you a taste of the heavens and leave you star struck! It could be the perfect ending to your day at the park- it is conveniently located in Stadtpark, Winterhude.

23. Tunnel Through A Prestigious Landmark

This 2,000-foot tunnel is every Hamburger's pride! Find its entrance marked by a majestic dome at Landungsbruecken.

Take the car lift, pedestrian lift or the staircase and descend 80 feet before you enter the Elbtunnel which runs below the river Elbe connecting the north and south parts of Hamburg. Inspect the artistic walls which depict life along the Elbe in the 1900s.

24. Appreciate Art On The Street

Watch the allies and lanes come alive through mimics, sand sculptors, soap-balloon blowers and cheerful musicians!

Among my pet artists are the bad-boy drummer usually at the main train station, the gentle old man wielding his sweet-sounding music box at Jungfernstieg and the hip-hop kids on Moenckebergstrasse.

Look around for the many make-up artists we have and try not to get startled when a "statue" smiles at you!

25. Grill By The Alster

Have a delicious barbeque or grill party as the Germans call it, out in the open. There are specified zones where grilling is permissible, so do stick to those. They're everywhere! Helpful hint- almost every super market has portable, disposable coal kits you can use and of course a delicious selection of foods just waiting to be barbequed! Plan your picnic and off you go!

Yourself At A Park

Hamburg's most artistically designed green spaces are called Stadtpark and Planten un Blomen. They stretch way beyond the eye can see and are a refreshing breath of freshness from the hustle and bustle of the city.

Check out various gardening styles, a musical fountain (at nights), life size chess games and a dozen other activities at each of these botanical beauties.

27. Party At The Reeperbahn

The Reeperbahn or the Kiez, is Hamburg's most famous or infamous

street, depending on which way you view it. In the past, ships docked

and sailors spilled onto the street to satisfy their many needs. You get

the idea! The street is filled with clubs, pubs, strip clubs, karaoke bars

and sex shops. No one discriminates and it's fairly normal to see a

gorgeous transvestite giving a guided tour. Start at the one euro bar, go

to the doll house, eat a Hessburger and appreciate the marvelous chaos

of the Kiez!

28. Get Yourself Some Wheels

Rent a state sponsored cycle- Stadtrad- the red bikes parked outside tube stations. You pay a few Euros for a lifetime membership and the first 30 minutes of every ride are always free. Thereafter you pay a few cents a minute. If you look for white boards with red writing, you'll spot the many cycle routes through the city.

29. Lead Yourself To Foodie Paradise

My two hot spots for delving into a dizzying choice of food cuisines are Schulterblatt in Sternschanze and Hansaplatz in St. Georg. These areas are home to exotic food tastes and types and you will not be disappointed! The varieties range from Indian Dosas and Samosas to Venezuelan Arepas and Romanian Polenta and Sarmale! Of course, there are others you might fancy more- Turkish, German, Italian, Mexican, Afghani, Syrian and Chinese.

30. Saunter Along The Lange Reihe

Located in St Georg, this is the Gay Street of Hamburg. Rainbows everywhere signal that everyone is welcome. Shop at chic boutiques, toast or enjoy cake at the iconic Cafe Gnosa or simply soak in the fancy friendly spirit of this street. Look for street festivals and flea markets, as the Lange Reihe hosts many colorful ones. The Aussenalster (outer lake) is a quick two minute distance from here by foot.

"Once a year, go someplace you've never been before." – Anon

31. Look For A Franzbroetchen

Hamburg's croissant. Or rather Hamburg's failed attempt at a croissant, which then took on an identity of its own. Today the Franz (French) broetchen (small bread) is an integral symbol of Hamburg's bakery scene. Enjoy it with powdered cinnamon and sugar or with crunchy nuts sprinkled all over.

32. Try A Water Sport

Take your pick of the many that Hamburg offers. On good wind days,

the Alster is peppered with sails. Go rowing, stand up paddling or wake

boarding depending on your preference and have viel Spass (lots of fun)

on the water! Ahoy!

33. Work Up A Sweat In Winter

Although Hamburg doesn't have heavy snowfall or mountains, it is big on winter sports. You can ice skate in the center and go snowboarding or skiing at either of the two snow domes. Sweating not your thing? Work on your beer biceps! Lift, drink, repeat!

34. Fly High On Adrenaline

Head over to the Dom. At your service thrice a year, the Dom (not a church in this case) is full of crazy rides, roller coasters, scary houses, sweet savories and tons of prizes. You'll find it by taking the tube (U3) to either Feldstrasse or St. Pauli. Keep your eyes open for their firework schedule, it's a pretty impressive one.

35. Gear Up For Gluehwein

The many Weihnachtsmarkts or Christmas markets in Hamburg, already up in November, transform it into a fairy tale wonderland. It's my favorite part of winter, and I get bewitched by tinsel and shiny lights. More importantly, you get to keep the chill away by drinking Gluehwein, which is red wine and spices served steaming hot. For non-alcoholic options, try Kinder (children's) punch. Don't forget to sample crepes (available all year around) and freshly roasted almonds.

36. Hope That Queen Mary Is In Town

Hamburg and The Queen Mary have an intimate relationship. The whole city celebrates when she's in town. In case you haven't caught on, I'm talking about the ship. The Harbour Birthday celebrated every May is a spectacular event with more than a million visitors. The pomp is around ship launches, parades, the unique tugboat ballet and spell-binding fireworks.

37. Strike A Yoga Pose

The city is teeming with yoga enthusiasts and you can find every possible yoga variety here. Just put out your mat in the park or join a drop-in class. In summer, you find several community yoga classes conducted on a donation basis. Flex those muscles and give them a well-deserved stretch!

38. Experience Hamburg The Alternative Way

The Gaengeviertal is Hamburg's hidden treasure, sitting between concrete giants within the city center. The initiative to "Komm in die Gaenge" (get into gear) converted a decaying district into an artist's haven. You now have a space filled with expressions of art, music, political and social ideas. Attend a workshop here or a party and see Hamburg's lesser known cultural and social side. One can get here by the U2 to Gaensemarkt.

39. Jump On The Festival Wagon

All year through there are dozens of local and international musicians performing in Hamburg. If you're lucky you can watch your favorite band perform.

One of my most cherished events is the Reeperbahn Festival held every September where upcoming artists take the floor and often blow your mind away!

40. Shop Until You Drop

The stores overflow with latest trends in fashion, technology, sports and every conceivable piece of equipment. Moenckebergstrasse, Jungfernstieg and Karolinviertal are hot spots for die hard shoppers. Even window shopping is quite a demanding activity! For groceries, you have local markets as well as brands such as Edeka, Aldi and Lidl.

"I love to travel, but hate to arrive." – Albert Einstein

41. Hop On A Boat

You can do a whole loop of 9 km along the Elbe or a short ride that costs a few euros. Check Alster Tourism at Jungfernstieg to book a tour of your choice. Or simply take the ferry from Landungsbruecken to Finkenwerder. PS- this short ride is usually included in your day ticket price.

42. Pay Tribute To Victims Of War

Look down along the pavements and you will see square brass plaques inscribed with names and dates. These Stolpersteine or stumbling stones mark the last place of residence of world war two victims. This art project was designed to keep memory of dark times alive and caution against it happening again.

43. Plan An Excursion To The Sea-Side

While Hamburg is a gem, it is surrounded by several other nuggets you could discover. Well connected by road and rail, make a day trip to:

Luebeck- a UNESCO World Heritage Site due to its Brick Gothic Architecture.

Bremerhaven- this idyllic city has mostly post-war architecture, however I found the Zoo most fascinating!

Kiel- one of Germany's major maritime centers and home to the largest sailing event in the world every June.

44. Flee To A Flohmarkt

Flohmarkts or Flea markets are a common sight in Hamburg both during the week and weekends. Reap the benefits of a farmer's market or check out the Flohschanze one that offers a wide range of articles from antics, to cycles, books and jewelry.

45. Spend A Day At The Zoo

This is a real treat for kids and adults alike. The Hagenpark Tierpark was the first ever in the 70s to introduce enclosures and moats instead of cages. Visit the walruses, the elephants and penguins and take a look at the tropical aquarium. Have fun watching the colorful flora and fauna this zoo has on offer.

46. Feel The Football Frenzy

Hamburg's two main Football clubs, HSV and St. Pauli are at logger heads with each other. They each have their own stadiums. The competition is fierce and the fans even fiercer. Go to a game if you have a strong heart and join in with the cheering chorus.

A battle cry you might hear on the field and in the audience, is: Hummel, Hummel! To which, the reply is Mors Mors! The origins of this phrase are rather colorful and worth looking up, if only for a laugh.

47. Zero In On Your Hamburger

This, my friend can be a highly individualistic choice. While most recommend Otto's Burger, The Burger Lab or Burgerlich, I had my best one at Currypapa. Go find yours! Oh, and it is still disputed about whether Hamburgers came from Hamburg or America.

48. Go Back To The Beatles' Beginning

Hamburg has had its share of artists in the making and the legendary Beatles were no exception. Visit the Beatles Platz at Grosser Freiheit on the Repperbahn where they played regularly. You can even take a Beatles Tour given by a local who lived through the 60s and 70s and has firsthand experience of the band in the making.

49. Speak At A Stammtisch

Roughly translated, a Stammtisch is a table at bars for regulars. A Stammtisch is a tradition passed down through the years where people with common interests meet and exchange ideas or simply have a nice conversation over drinks. Topics range from languages, food and hobbies to gaming and travel. The English Stammtisch or E-Tisch meets up thrice a month to eat, drink and yes, speak English.

50. Attend An Event At The Fabrik

This former machine-parts factory is now a hip cultural center. Don't let the outer façade fool you. The Fabrik has on offer debates, films, concerts, flea markets; and even played host to Nirvana! Head off to Altona and discover how the new generation is transforming former industrial spaces for cultural events.

> TOURIST

GREATER THAN A TOURIST

Visit GreaterThanATourist.com
http://GreaterThanATourist.com

Sign up for the Greater Than a Tourist Newsletter
http://eepurl.com/cxspyf

Follow us on Facebook:
https://www.facebook.com/GreaterThanATourist

Follow us on Pinterest:
http://pinterest.com/GreaterThanATourist

Follow us on Instagram:
http://Instagram.com/GreaterThanATourist

> TOURIST

GREATER THAN A TOURIST

Please leave your honest review of this book on Amazon and Goodreads. Thank you.

We appreciate your positive and negative feedback as we try to provide tourist guidance in their next trip from a local.

> TOURIST

GREATER THAN A TOURIST

You can find Greater Than a Tourist books on Amazon.

GREATER THAN A TOURIST

WHERE WILL YOU TRAVEL TO NEXT?

> TOURIST

GREATER THAN A TOURIST

Our Story

Traveling is a passion of this series creator. She studied abroad in college, and for their honeymoon Lisa and her husband toured Europe. During her travels to Malta, an older man tried to give her some advice based on his own experience living on the island since he was a young boy. She thought he was just trying to sell her something. When traveling to some places she was wary to talk to locals because she was afraid that they weren't being genuine. She created this book series to give you as a tourist an inside view on the place you are exploring and the ability to learn what locals would like to tell tourist.   A topic that they are very passionate about.

> TOURIST

GREATER THAN A TOURIST

Notes

19794827R00060

Printed in Poland
by Amazon Fulfillment
Poland Sp. z o.o., Wrocław